Becoming A Parent

Lianne Mcmahon

BookLeaf Publishing
India | USA | UK

Presentation by *BookLeaf Publishing*

Web: www.bookleafpub.com

E-mail: info@bookleafpub.com

ISBN: 9789357211871

First edition 2023

DEDICATION

For Isla xx

Hello Little One

A tiny tadpole,

Growing away,

And cooking in my tummy.

A 'bun in the oven'

They say.

So tiny

So vulnerable

So loved

Already.

We've got to be careful

As it is so early.

It's easy to get excited

And plan the next stages

But we must pause this

And wait for the first scan.

No one tells you how hard

This wait really is.

How much you want to

Tell everyone your news.

And then you think back

To the little dot

In your tummy.

Once we see you

Little one,

Then we can share you

With the world.

For My Daughter

Little fingers

Little toes

A big heart

And a clever mind.

You're so loved baby girl

You've filled us with a whirl

Of love and warmth

That we are full to the

Brim

And waiting to overflow

With all our love for you ❤

The Cries

Which cry is this?

Are you hungry, sleepy,

wet, sad, or in pain?

Sometimes it's just the need

For a cuddle

And this will soothe you.

But sometimes it's pain

From the colic

And we can't help you.

It's heartbreaking.

I'm sorry your tummy is hurting

Mummy is trying to help

But at 2 weeks old

There's not much we can give you.

I'll continue to rock you,

Cuddle you,

Sing to you

And love you.

In the hope this will

Soothe you

Back to sleep

Eventually.

Love you baby girl ❤

Becoming Dad

Watching you become daddy

Is the most beautiful thing

You're amazing, calm, loving

And besotted with her already.

Your kind words

Gigantic hugs

A chest that's fit to sleep on

And the warmth you give

Are appreciated by our little one.

She loves you

And I love you even more

After seeing this journey

To fatherhood.

Well done daddy

Loving You

That first cry filled us with tears;

Relief is all we felt.

We were so glad you'd arrived

And your little face told us

You were happy and content.

We loved you immediately.

Your little nose

Little face

And the most beautiful blue eyes

Continue to make us melt

Everyday.

Gorgeous baby Isla

You were the only baby to sleep

While all the others were crying

You found comfort in mummy's arms

While daddy was away.

And we waited

Just the one day

And then we brought you home

And snuggled

All day.

Dream Big

My heart is exploding

And my mind is overloaded

With how much I care for you.

How can something so little

Fill me with so much emotion?

My baby girl, you are my world.

My one and only everything

In just a split second

You became the most important person

To me.

I love you dearly baby girl.

You make me proud everyday;

I love watching you grow and play.

You're so clever and so strong

I can see you're determined

To prove everyone wrong.

A strong willed girl

Taking on the world

And striving only for the best

Never taking any rest

Until you achieve your

Wildest dreams.

Night Time

Night time is the hardest.

While you sleep well

And through the night

Mummy misses you

Even though

You're right by her side.

Every movement I wake

Every breath I count

Each twitch I hope

That your dreams are happy.

And then the morning arrives

And you give me the biggest smile

My anxiety of the night is gone

And I enjoy another day with you ❤

A Note To My Daughter

My darling girl

You are so beautiful

Your smile warms my heart

You can do anything you want baby girl

Don't let anything get in your way

Keep that determined mind going

Push boundaries

Open up your feelings and

Show everyone your whole true self

At all times

Because

You are amazing

And one of a kind.

Joy

When I think back to the moment

We found out about you

The secrets we had to keep

Yet loving you all the way through.

From the little dot

To the little tot

We love and see every day.

The journey of nothing but joy

And while we had to be coy

Before we announced your arrival.

Now, we get to share you

With the world.

Each smile, each noise,

Each month you grow

And we'll always love you

More than you know.

Oh Baby Girl

Your smile melts me

You do love a sing song

With mummy

I'd sing to you all day long

If that smile stays shining brightly.

We sing and play,

We laugh and dance

Everyday.

Just to keep you

Smiling.

You'll be a heartbreaker

With that smile and those eyes

And probably a trouble maker

With that mischievous grin

Such a happy girl

In this big wide world

Never stop smiling!

Singing

Learning the nursery rhymes

To see your face light up

Whether it's

Twinkling little stars

An itsy bitsy spider

Or pop goes the weasel.

We love a song

Because you smile so wide

With each one sung.

Telling you stories of

Humpty Dumpty,

Georgie Porgie,

Singing about puddings and pies.

The Teddy Bears picnic

And all the stars in the sky.

Jack and Jill

And their pale of water

The Ugly Duckling

And the piggy that came after.

These are the stories

To make you smile.

To the moon and back

My darling

It's all worthwhile.

Cuddles

10 little fingers
And 10 little toes
A cute little smile
And a button nose.

The ooos and ahhhs
And babbles aplenty
Enjoying cuddles
And the bottles are empty.

Naps with a dummy
And snuggles with mummy
Laughter and playing
With daddy swaying.

All cosy and warm

With no lights on.

It's bedtime baby girl

Time to say goodnight to the world.

Bath Time

Bath time and playtime

Bath time and laughter

Bath time and bubbles

And excitement for what comes after

And that's...

Lots and lots of snuggles!

Rubber ducks and sprinkles

From the running shower.

Sponges and shampoo

Scrubbing for half an hour.

Squeaky clean and ready for bed

Toasty and snug

Wrapped up nice and warm

Like a great big hug.

Wonder

Wondering what's going on

In that little brain of yours,

You seem to be so fascinated

with the world around you.

Your eyes go wide with wonder.

Is it exciting what you see?

The bright colours and

Smiling faces must brighten your day

As we babble and play

Reading and singing to you

And then watching and waiting

For your reaction.

Because that smile

Is a mile wide and growing.

Your face lights up with joy

It's almost glowing.

Don't worry baby girl

We want to keep your smile there

And with a story, a dance or a tickle

We will show you how much we care.

Motherhood

Motherhood is a journey.

A treacherous journey

With a roller coaster of emotions

That never leave you

Once the baby arrives.

The slightest sad moment

Can leave you in floods of tears

And your heart

Breaks

Just a little

Each time your baby cries.

It's one of the hardest challenges

Life can bring.

Yet also the most rewarding

As the love received by something

So small

And yet so mighty.

Fills you up from the top

To your toes

With love and affection

That overspills

In all directions.

As you tangle your way through

To manage those emotions,

This tiny human

Is full of devotion

To you.

Rocking

We will rock you,

Love you, hug you.

We will rock you,

Kiss you, swaddle you

Until you fall asleep.

Keeping on rocking

To comfort and cuddle

And rock, rock, rock

So that your tears stop

And you fall fast asleep.

Keep on swaying while you're laying

In mummy or daddy's arms

Feeling safe from harm

And helping your journey

To the land of slumber.

We will rock and sway

To keep those tears away

For yet another day.

The Worry

Something I wish I'd been told

About becoming a parent

Is the worry about food.

Is she getting enough?

Is it too much?

How many times should she feed?

Which milk is the best way to go?

I managed 6 weeks of pumping

As she never latched.

6 weeks of breast milk

To give her as much of me

As possible.

And then our journey of weighing,

Milk experimentation,

And consultants began.

The worry of her weight

Weighing down on my mind.

I just want her to be healthy

And not have to worry whether she

Takes all of the next bottle.

At 3 months she's growing, rolling over,

Laughing, smiling, sitting up with help

And yet she's monitored

Because she doesn't follow their 'curve'.

This worry, eats away at my brain

Digging at the neurons

Until I snap.

But she's still growing

Just... too slowly and not to their liking.

I think she's perfect

But the monitoring creates anxiety.

Anxiety of food.

The feeding journey for babies

Is the hardest part so far.

And I wish somebody had warned me.

A Change in us

The positive little changes

That you have made to our lives

Are heartwarming.

Baby girl you have

Turned our world

Upside down

And yet I wouldn't change a thing

Because you're adorable when sleeping.

You make us laugh, cry and grin

With every expression you make within.

Although everything is now

Topsy Turvey

We are really enjoying

This journey.

Being a parent is tough

And we feel pretty rough

When being woken up in the night

Our eyes can't take the early light.

We squint, moan and frown

And pray that you'll go back down

And snuggle in your cot

And so we rock you

Back to sleep

And then we watch you

Sleeping

And with each breath

We thank our lucky stars

That you're safe, beautiful and can rest.

Firsts

You're our first baby

And we'll experience

So many firsts with you.

Your first smile

To warm our hearts.

Your first laugh

To make us melt.

Your first words

To get us excited.

Your first roll

To watch you grow.

Your first Christmas

To see our family shine.

Your first crawl

To begin your journey.

Your first steps

To join us

Hand in hand

And explore the world

Together as a family

Of three.

My Wishes For You

I wish that your future be bright

That you'll always find the light

In any given situation.

I wish that you are content

No matter what you do

And that any dream you may have

Will come true.

I wish that you'll come to me

Whenever you need help

And not be afraid

To ask when unsure.

I wish that you will know

When to be selfless and

When to be selfish

Because sometimes YOU matter most.

I wish that your mind stays free

From negative thoughts and worries

And that you'll enjoy life

And share your joy with others.

I wish for your smile to never fade

And for your hugs to remain the same.

And I wish for you to be happy

No matter where life takes you

And for your happiness to shine brightly

So that others become happy from you!

Time

I know time will go quickly

As I watch you grow

And wait for the next milestone

Which comes so easily.

Soon you'll be walking

And learning on your own

The world will get you talking

And then you'll be leaving home.

The future will arrive

Too quickly to notice

From crawling

To dancing

In the blink of an eye

And I'll think back

To when I wished

For your next trick:

Sitting up, rolling over,

Walking or running.

Instead I should enjoy

The stage you're at now.

Because before I know it

This will be gone

And my baby girl

Is no longer my baby any more

As you become a woman.

I'm proud of you already darling

But time goes so fast

So let me enjoy this moment

These cuddles need to last.

Love you baby girl xx

www.ingramcontent.com/pod-product-compliance
Lightning Source LLC
Chambersburg PA
CBHW051741130826
49812CB00033B/959
* 9 7 8 9 3 5 7 2 1 1 8 7 1 *